CONTENTS

QUICK & EASY
CROWD PLEASERS

Sweet Fruit Dip

PREP: 10 min. | **TOTAL:** 1 hour 10 min. | **MAKES:** 16 servings, 2 Tbsp. each.

---

4 oz. (½ of 8-oz. pkg.) PHILADELPHIA Cream Cheese, softened

1 cup whole berry cranberry sauce

1 cup thawed COOL WHIP Whipped Topping

BEAT cream cheese and cranberry sauce with electric mixer on medium speed until well blended. Gently stir in COOL WHIP; cover.

REFRIGERATE at least 1 hour or until ready to serve.

SERVE with strawberries, red and green grapes, pineapple, kiwi or pears, cut into bite-size pieces for dipping.

Fun Idea: This dip is great spooned over individual servings of cut-up fresh fruit.

White Chocolate-Raspberry Torte

PREP: 20 min. | **TOTAL:** 3 hours 20 min. | **MAKES:** 12 servings.

1 pkg. (4 oz.) BAKER'S White Chocolate, melted

1 pkg. (8 oz.) PHILADELPHIA Cream Cheese, softened

1 cup cold milk

1 pkg. (3.4 oz.) JELL-O Vanilla Flavor Instant Pudding

2 cups thawed COOL WHIP Whipped Topping, divided

1 pkg. (10.5 oz.) frozen pound cake, partially thawed, cut into 30 thin slices

¼ cup raspberry jam, warmed

½ cup fresh raspberries

BEAT chocolate and cream cheese with mixer until blended. Gradually beat in milk. Add dry pudding mix; beat until well blended. Whisk in 1 cup COOL WHIP.

ARRANGE 10 cake slices on bottom of 9-inch round pan lined with plastic wrap; brush with half the jam.

COVER with half the pudding mixture. Repeat all layers. Top with remaining cake.

REFRIGERATE 3 hours. Invert dessert onto plate; remove pan and plastic wrap. Top with remaining COOL WHIP and berries.

Special Extra: Use additional 1 oz. of BAKER'S White Chocolate to make chocolate curls.

Jazz It Up: Garnish with fresh mint leaves.

Variation: Prepare using BAKER'S Semi-Sweet Chocolate and 1 pkg. (3.9 oz.) JELL-O Chocolate Instant Pudding, and adding ½ cup more COOL WHIP to the pudding mixture before using as directed.

Rocky Road No-Bake Cheesecake

PREP: 15 min. | **TOTAL:** 4 hours 15 min. | **MAKES:** 10 servings, 1 slice each.

- **3** oz. BAKER'S Semi-Sweet Chocolate, divided
- **2** pkg. (8 oz. each) PHILADELPHIA Cream Cheese, softened
- ⅓ cup sugar
- ¼ cup milk
- **2** cups thawed COOL WHIP Whipped Topping
- ¾ cup JET-PUFFED Miniature Marshmallows
- ⅓ cup chopped PLANTERS COCKTAIL Peanuts
- **1** ready-to-use chocolate flavor crumb crust (6 oz.)

MICROWAVE 1 oz. chocolate in small microwaveable bowl on HIGH 1 min.; stir until chocolate is completely melted. Set aside.

BEAT cream cheese, sugar and milk in large bowl with electric mixer on medium speed until well blended. Add melted chocolate; mix well. Gently stir in COOL WHIP, marshmallows and peanuts. Coarsely chop remaining 2 oz. chocolate; stir into cream cheese mixture. Spoon into crust.

REFRIGERATE 4 hours or until set. Garnish as desired. Store leftover pie in refrigerator.

Coffee-Drizzled Cream Cheese Pie

PREP: 15 min. | **TOTAL:** 2 hours 15 min. | **MAKES:** 8 servings.

- **1** pkg. (8 oz.) PHILADELPHIA Cream Cheese, softened

- **⅓** cup sugar

- **½** cup milk

- **2** Tbsp. MAXWELL HOUSE INTERNATIONAL CAFÉ Suisse Mocha Café

- **1** ready-to-use graham cracker crumb crust (6 oz.)

- **1** tub (8 oz.) COOL WHIP Whipped Topping, thawed

BEAT cream cheese in medium bowl until creamy. Gradually add sugar, mixing until well blended. Stir in milk. Remove ¼ cup of the cream cheese mixture; place in small bowl. Stir in flavored instant coffee mix. Drizzle 1 Tbsp. of the coffee-flavored cream cheese mixture onto bottom of crust. Set remaining coffee-flavored cream cheese mixture aside.

STIR COOL WHIP gently into remaining plain cream cheese mixture, stirring just until combined. Spoon into crust. Drizzle with remaining coffee-flavored cream cheese mixture. Swirl knife gently through mixtures several times for marble effect.

REFRIGERATE 2 hours or until set. Store leftover pie in refrigerator.

Chocolate-Peppermint Striped Delight

PREP: 30 min. | **TOTAL:** 4 hours 30 min. | **MAKES:** 24 servings.

---

45 vanilla wafers, finely crushed (about 1½ cups)

¼ cup butter, melted

½ cup sugar, divided

1 pkg. (8 oz.) PHILADELPHIA Cream Cheese, softened

3 cups plus 2 Tbsp. cold milk, divided

¼ cup finely crushed candy canes

1 tub (12 oz.) COOL WHIP Whipped Topping, thawed, divided

2 pkg. (3.9 oz. each) JELL-O Chocolate Instant Pudding

¼ cup coarsely crushed candy canes

MIX wafer crumbs, butter and 2 Tbsp. sugar; press onto bottom of 13×9-inch pan. Refrigerate until ready to use.

BEAT cream cheese, remaining sugar and 2 Tbsp. milk in medium bowl until blended. Stir in finely crushed candy canes. Add 1¼ cups COOL WHIP; mix well. Spread over crust.

BEAT dry pudding mixes and remaining 3 cups milk with whisk 2 min.; pour over cream cheese layer. Let stand 5 min. or until thickened. Cover with remaining COOL WHIP.

REFRIGERATE 4 hours. Top with coarsely crushed candy canes just before serving.

How to Easily Cut Dessert to Serve: Place dessert in freezer about 1 hour before cutting into squares to serve.

Mounds of Joy Whipped Pie

PREP: 50 min. | **TOTAL:** 50 min. | **MAKES:** 6 servings.

1 pkg. (8 oz.) PHILADELPHIA Cream Cheese, softened

1 cup cream of coconut

1 pkg. (3.9 oz.) JELL-O Cheesecake Flavor Instant Pudding

14 oz. frozen sweetened flaked coconut, divide in ½ and toast ½

2 tubs (8 oz. each) COOL WHIP Whipped Topping, divided

1 chocolate cookie crumb pie crust (6 oz.)

Hard-shell chocolate ice cream topping (optional)

6 mini chocolate-coated coconut and almond candy bars

BEAT cream cheese and cream of coconut until smooth and creamy. Add dry pudding mix; beat until well blended.

ADD ½ thawed, but cold, coconut. Mix well. Fold in 1 tub COOL WHIP.

POUR half the pudding mixture into crust. Drizzle with hard-shell chocolate ice cream topping, if desired. Cover with remaining pudding mixture.

MIX ¾ cup toasted coconut with remaining COOL WHIP; spread over pie.

TOP with candy bars and remaining toasted coconut.

FREEZE 30 min. or refrigerate 45 min. or until firm.

How to Toast Coconut: Toast coconut on plate in microwave until evenly browned. Stir often to prevent burning. WATCH CLOSELY. If you wish to use the coconut without toasting, that is also acceptable.

PHILADELPHIA SNACK DELIGHTS
Turtle Dessert Dip

PREP: 5 min. | **TOTAL:** 5 min. | **MAKES:** 10 servings, 2 Tbsp. each.

---

1 tub (8 oz.) PHILADELPHIA SNACK DELIGHTS Milk Chocolate

2 Tbsp. caramel ice cream topping

2 Tbsp. chopped PLANTERS Pecans

SPOON PHILADELPHIA SNACK DELIGHTS into serving bowl.

DRIZZLE with caramel topping; top with nuts.

Serving Suggestion: Serve with pretzel crisps, apple slices and/or graham crackers.

Peanut-Chocolate Mud Pie Squares

PREP: 25 min. | **TOTAL:** 12 hours 25 min. | **MAKES:** 16 servings.

---

20 chocolate sandwich cookies, finely crushed (about 1⅔ cups), divided

¼ cup butter, melted

1 tub (8 oz.) PHILADELPHIA Cream Cheese Spread

½ cup PLANTERS Creamy Peanut Butter

¼ cup sugar

1 tub (8 oz.) COOL WHIP Whipped Topping, thawed, divided

1 pkg. (3.9 oz.) JELL-O Chocolate Instant Pudding

1½ cups cold milk

¼ cup coarsely chopped PLANTERS COCKTAIL Peanuts

LINE 9-inch square pan with plastic wrap, with ends of wrap extending over sides. Mix 1¼ cups cookie crumbs and butter; press onto bottom of prepared pan. Refrigerate until ready to use.

BEAT cream cheese spread, peanut butter and sugar in medium bowl with mixer until well blended. Gently stir in 1½ cups COOL WHIP; spread over crust. Top with ¼ cup of the remaining cookie crumbs.

BEAT dry pudding mix and milk in same bowl with mixer on low speed 2 min. Stir in remaining COOL WHIP; spoon over crumb mixture. Top with remaining crumbs and nuts.

FREEZE overnight. Remove dessert from freezer 20 min. before serving; let stand at room temperature to soften slightly. Use plastic wrap handles to remove dessert from pan before cutting into squares.

Tiramisu Bowl

PREP: 20 min. | **TOTAL:** 2 hours 20 min. | **MAKES:** 16 servings, about ⅔ cup each.

1 pkg. (8 oz.) PHILADELPHIA Cream Cheese, softened

2 pkg. (3.4 oz. each) JELL-O Vanilla Flavor Instant Pudding

3 cups cold milk

1 tub (8 oz.) COOL WHIP Whipped Topping, thawed, divided

48 vanilla wafers

½ cup brewed strong MAXWELL HOUSE Coffee, cooled, divided

2 oz. BAKER'S Semi-Sweet Chocolate, grated

1 cup fresh raspberries

BEAT cream cheese with mixer until creamy. Add dry pudding mixes and milk; beat 2 min. Gently stir in COOL WHIP.

LINE 2½-qt. bowl with 24 wafers; drizzle with ¼ cup coffee. Top with half each of the pudding mixture and chocolate. Repeat all layers.

TOP with remaining COOL WHIP and raspberries. Refrigerate 2 hours.

How to Easily Grate Chocolate: Before grating the chocolate, microwave it on HIGH for 10 sec. or just until slightly softened.

SUPREME CAKES

Banana Split "Cake"

PREP: 15 min. | **TOTAL:** 5 hours 15 min. | **MAKES:** 24 servings.

1½ cups graham cracker crumbs

1 cup sugar, divided

⅓ cup butter, melted

2 pkg. (8 oz. each) PHILADELPHIA Cream Cheese, softened

1 can (20 oz.) crushed pineapple in juice, drained

6 bananas, divided

2 pkg. (3.4 oz. each) JELL-O Vanilla Flavor Instant Pudding

2 cups cold milk

2 cups thawed COOL WHIP Whipped Topping, divided

1 oz. BAKER'S Semi-Sweet Chocolate, shaved into curls

MIX graham crumbs, ¼ cup sugar and butter; press onto bottom of 13×9-inch pan. Freeze 10 min.

BEAT cream cheese and remaining sugar with mixer until well blended. Spread carefully over crust; top with pineapple. Slice 4 bananas; arrange over pineapple.

BEAT dry pudding mixes and milk in medium bowl with whisk 2 min. Stir in 1 cup COOL WHIP; spread over banana layer in pan. Top with remaining COOL WHIP. Refrigerate 5 hours.

SLICE remaining bananas just before serving; arrange over dessert. Garnish with chocolate curls.

Substitute: Substitute 1 cup chopped PLANTERS Pecans for the shaved chocolate.

Snowball Cake

PREP: 15 min. | **TOTAL:** 2 hours 20 min. | **MAKES:** 16 servings.

1 pkg. (2-layer size) devil's food cake mix

1 pkg. (8 oz.) PHILADELPHIA Cream Cheese, softened

1 egg

2 tbsp. granulated sugar

1 pkg. (3.4 oz.) JELL-O Vanilla Flavor Instant Pudding

¼ cup powdered sugar

1 cup cold milk

1 tub (8 oz.) COOL WHIP Whipped Topping, thawed

1 cup BAKER'S ANGEL FLAKE Coconut

HEAT oven to 350°F.

PREPARE cake batter, in 2½-qt. ovenproof bowl, as directed on package; scrape side of bowl. Beat cream cheese, egg and granulated sugar until well blended; spoon into center of batter in bowl.

BAKE 1 hour 5 min. or until toothpick inserted in center comes out clean. Cool in bowl 10 min.

LOOSEN cake from bowl with knife; invert onto wire rack. Remove bowl. Cool cake completely. Beat dry pudding mix, powdered sugar and milk in medium bowl with whisk 2 min. Stir in COOL WHIP. Refrigerate until ready to use.

PLACE cake on plate; frost with pudding mixture. Cover with coconut. Keep refrigerated.

Dark Chocolate-Hazelnut Souffle

PREP: 10 min. | **TOTAL:** 55 min. | **MAKES:** 6 servings.

1 tsp. butter

½ cup plus 1 Tbsp. sugar, divided

6 eggs

1 tub (8 oz.) PHILADELPHIA Cream Cheese Spread

1 Tbsp. hazelnut-flavored liqueur

3 oz. BAKER'S Bittersweet Chocolate, melted

2 Tbsp. chopped hazelnuts, toasted

HEAT oven to 350°F.

GREASE bottom and side of 1-qt. souffle dish or casserole with butter; sprinkle with 1 Tbsp. sugar.

BLEND eggs, cream cheese spread, remaining sugar, liqueur and chocolate in blender 30 sec. or until smooth. Blend on high speed 15 sec. Pour into souffle dish.

BAKE 40 to 45 min. or until puffed and lightly browned. Sprinkle with nuts; serve immediately.

Special Extra: Serve topped with mixed berries.

Variation: Substitute 1 tsp. almond extract for the liqueur and PLANTERS Slivered Almonds for the chopped hazelnuts.

Pumpkin Spice Cake with Brown Sugar Frosting

PREP: 20 min. | **TOTAL:** 1 hour 50 min. | **MAKES:** 16 servings.

- **1** pkg. (2-layer size) spice cake mix

- **1** cup water

- **1** cup canned pumpkin

- **⅓** cup oil

- **3** eggs

- **¾** cup chopped PLANTERS Walnuts

- **1** pkg. (8 oz.) PHILADELPHIA Neufchâtel Cheese, softened

- **⅓** cup packed dark brown sugar

- **1** cup thawed COOL WHIP LITE Whipped Topping

HEAT oven to 350°F.

BEAT first 5 ingredients in large bowl with mixer 2 min. or until well blended. Stir in nuts. Pour into 13×9-inch pan sprayed with cooking spray.

BAKE 30 to 32 min. or until toothpick inserted in center comes out clean. Cool completely.

BEAT Neufchâtel and sugar in small bowl with mixer until well blended. Add COOL WHIP; mix well. Spread over cake.

How to Store: Store frosted cake in refrigerator.

How to Store Remaining Canned Pumpkin: Remaining canned pumpkin can be stored in airtight container in freezer up to 3 months before using as desired.

Tuxedo Cake

PREP: 30 min. | **TOTAL:** 1 hour 43 min. | **MAKES:** 16 servings.

---

1 pkg. (2-layer size) devil's food cake mix

1 pkg. (3.9 oz.) JELL-O Chocolate Instant Pudding

1½ pkg. (8 oz. each) PHILADELPHIA Cream Cheese, softened

½ cup butter, softened

1½ tsp. vanilla

6 cups powdered sugar

½ of 8-oz. tub COOL WHIP Whipped Topping (Do not thaw.)

3 oz. BAKER'S Semi-Sweet Chocolate, divided

1 oz. BAKER'S White Chocolate

HEAT oven to 350°F.

PREPARE cake batter and bake as directed on package for 2 (9-inch) round cake layers, blending dry pudding mix into batter before pouring into prepared pans. Cool 10 min. Loosen cakes from sides of pans with knife. Invert onto wire racks; gently remove pans. Cool cakes completely.

MEANWHILE, beat cream cheese, butter and vanilla in large bowl with mixer until blended. Gradually beat in sugar.

CUT each cake layer horizontally in half. Stack on plate, spreading ¾ cup cream cheese frosting between each layer. Spread remaining frosting onto top and side of cake.

MICROWAVE COOL WHIP and 2 oz. semi-sweet chocolate in microwaveable bowl on HIGH 1½ min., stirring after 1 min.; stir until chocolate is completely melted and mixture is well blended. Cool 5 min. Pour over cake, letting excess drip down side. Use vegetable peeler to make curls from remaining semi-sweet and white chocolates. Use to garnish cheesecake just before serving.

CLASSIC
CHEESECAKES

White Chocolate-Cherry Pecan Cheesecake

PREP: 30 min. | **TOTAL:** 6 hours 30 min. | **MAKES:** 16 servings.

---

1 cup PLANTERS Pecan Halves, toasted, divided

1½ cups graham cracker crumbs

¼ cup sugar

¼ cup margarine or butter, melted

3 pkg. (8 oz. each) PHILADELPHIA Cream Cheese, softened

1 can (14 oz.) sweetened condensed milk

1½ pkg. (4 oz. each) BAKER'S White Chocolate, melted

2 tsp. vanilla, divided

4 eggs

1 can (21 oz.) cherry pie filling

1 cup thawed COOL WHIP Whipped Topping

HEAT oven to 300°F.

RESERVE 16 of the pecan halves. Finely chop remaining pecans; mix with graham crumbs, sugar and margarine. Press firmly onto bottom of 9-inch springform pan.

BEAT cream cheese in large bowl with electric mixer on medium speed until creamy. Gradually beat in sweetened condensed milk until well blended. Add chocolate and 1 tsp. of the vanilla; mix well. Add eggs, 1 at a time, mixing on low speed just until blended. Pour over crust.

BAKE 1 hour or until center is almost set. Run knife around rim of pan to loosen cake; cool before removing rim. Refrigerate 4 hours or overnight.

MIX pie filling and remaining vanilla; spoon over cheesecake. Top with COOL WHIP and reserved pecan halves.

White Chocolate Cheesecake

PREP: 40 min. | **TOTAL:** 7 hours 5 min. | **MAKES:** 16 servings.

½ cup butter, softened

¾ cup sugar, divided

1½ tsp. vanilla, divided

1 cup flour

4 pkg. (8 oz. each) PHILADELPHIA Cream Cheese, softened

3 pkg. (4 oz. each) BAKER'S White Chocolate, melted, slightly cooled

4 eggs

2 cups fresh raspberries

HEAT oven to 325°F.

BEAT butter, ¼ cup sugar, and ½ tsp. vanilla in small bowl with mixer until light and fluffy. Gradually beat in flour until well blended; press onto bottom of 9-inch springform pan. Prick with fork. Bake 25 min. or until edge is lightly browned.

BEAT cream cheese, remaining sugar and vanilla in large bowl with mixer until well blended. Add chocolate; mix well. Add eggs, 1 at a time, beating on low speed after each addition just until blended. Pour over crust.

BAKE 55 min. to 1 hour or until center is almost set. Run knife around rim of pan to loosen cake; cool before removing rim. Refrigerate 4 hours. Top with raspberries just before serving.

White-Chocolate Macadamia Cheesecake: Prepare as directed, stirring ¾ cup chopped PLANTERS Macadamias into the batter before pouring over crust and baking as directed.

PHILADELPHIA New York Cheesecake

PREP: 15 min. | **TOTAL:** 5 hours 25 min. | **MAKES:** 16 servings.

21 chocolate sandwich cookies, finely crushed (about 2 cups)

3 Tbsp. butter or margarine, melted

5 pkg. (8 oz. each) PHILADELPHIA Cream Cheese, softened

1 cup sugar

3 Tbsp. flour

1 Tbsp. vanilla

1 cup BREAKSTONE'S or KNUDSEN Sour Cream

4 eggs

1 can (21 oz.) cherry pie filling

HEAT oven to 325°F.

LINE 13×9-inch pan with foil, with ends of foil extending over sides. Mix cookie crumbs and butter; press onto bottom of pan.

BEAT cream cheese, sugar, flour and vanilla with mixer until well blended. Add sour cream; mix well. Add eggs, 1 at a time, mixing on low speed after each just until blended. Pour over crust.

BAKE 40 min. or until center is almost set. Cool completely. Refrigerate 4 hours. Use foil handles to lift cheesecake from pan before cutting to serve. Top with pie filling.

Creamy Lemon Squares

PREP: 25 min. | **TOTAL:** 3 hours 53 min. | **MAKES:** 16 servings.

---

20 reduced-fat vanilla wafers, finely crushed (about ¾ cup)

½ cup flour

¼ cup packed brown sugar

¼ cup cold margarine

1 pkg. (8 oz.) PHILADELPHIA Neufchâtel Cheese, softened

1 cup granulated sugar

2 eggs

2 Tbsp. flour

3 Tbsp. lemon zest, divided

¼ cup fresh lemon juice

¼ cup CALUMET Baking Powder

2 tsp. powdered sugar

HEAT oven to 350°F.

LINE 8-inch square pan with foil, with ends of foil extending over sides. Mix first 3 ingredients in medium bowl. Cut in margarine with pastry blender or 2 knives until mixture resembles coarse crumbs; press onto bottom of prepared pan. Bake 15 min.

MEANWHILE, beat Neufchâtel and granulated sugar with mixer until well blended. Add eggs and 2 Tbsp. flour; mix well. Blend in 1 Tbsp. lemon zest, juice and baking powder; pour over crust.

BAKE 25 to 28 min. or until center is set. Cool completely. Refrigerate 2 hours. Sprinkle with powdered sugar and remaining zest just before serving.

PHILADELPHIA Brownie Cheesecake

PREP: 10 min. | **TOTAL:** 6 hours | **MAKES:** 16 servings.

---

1 pkg. (19 to 21 oz.) brownie mix (13×9-inch pan size)

4 pkg. (8 oz. each) PHILADELPHIA Cream Cheese, softened

1 cup sugar

1 tsp. vanilla

½ cup BREAKSTONE'S or KNUDSEN Sour Cream

3 eggs

2 oz. BAKER'S Semi-Sweet Chocolate

HEAT oven to 325°F.

PREPARE brownie batter as directed on package; pour into 13×9-inch pan sprayed with cooking spray. Bake 25 min. or until top is shiny and center is almost set.

MEANWHILE, beat cream cheese, sugar and vanilla in large bowl with mixer until well blended. Add sour cream; mix well. Add eggs, 1 at a time, mixing on low speed after each just until blended. Gently pour over brownie layer in pan. (Filling will come almost to top of pan.)

BAKE 40 min. or until center is almost set. Run knife or metal spatula around edges of pan to loosen sides; cool. Refrigerate 4 hours.

MELT chocolate as directed on package; drizzle over cheesecake. Refrigerate 15 min. or until chocolate is firm.

PHILADELPHIA New York-Style Sour Cream-Topped Cheesecake

PREP: 15 min. | **TOTAL:** 5 hours 5 min. | **MAKES:** 16 servings.

1½ cups graham cracker crumbs

¼ cup butter, melted

1¼ cups sugar, divided

4 pkg. (8 oz. each) PHILADELPHIA Cream Cheese, softened

2 tsp. vanilla, divided

1 container (16 oz.) BREAKSTONE'S or KNUDSEN Sour Cream, divided

4 eggs

2 cups fresh strawberries, sliced

HEAT oven to 325°F.

LINE 13×9-inch pan with foil, with ends extending over sides of pan. Mix graham crumbs, butter and 2 Tbsp. sugar; press onto bottom of pan. Beat cream cheese, 1 cup of remaining sugar and 1 tsp. vanilla in large bowl with mixer until well blended. Add 1 cup sour cream; mix well. Add eggs, 1 at a time, beating on low speed after each just until blended. Pour over crust.

BAKE 40 min. or until center is almost set. Mix remaining sour cream, sugar and vanilla; carefully spread over cheesecake. Bake 10 min. Cool completely. Refrigerate 4 hours. Use foil handles to lift cheesecake from pan just before serving; top with berries.

Substitute: Substitute 1½ cups finely crushed chocolate sandwich cookies for the graham cracker crumbs.

Cappuccino Cheesecake

PREP: 25 min. | **TOTAL:** 6 hours 35 min. | **MAKES:** 16 servings.

1½ cups finely chopped PLANTERS Walnuts

3 Tbsp. butter or margarine, melted

2 Tbsp. sugar

4 pkg. (8 oz. each) PHILADELPHIA Cream Cheese, softened

1 cup sugar

3 Tbsp. flour

4 eggs

1 cup BREAKSTONE'S or KNUDSEN Sour Cream

1 Tbsp. MAXWELL HOUSE Instant Coffee

¼ tsp. ground cinnamon

¼ cup boiling water

1½ cups thawed COOL WHIP Whipped Topping

HEAT oven to 325°F.

MIX nuts, butter and 2 Tbsp. sugar; press onto bottom of 9-inch springform pan. Bake 10 min. Remove from oven; cool. Increase oven temperature to 450°F.

BEAT cream cheese, 1 cup sugar and flour with mixer until well blended. Add eggs, 1 at a time, mixing on low speed after each just until blended. Blend in sour cream.

DISSOLVE instant coffee with cinnamon in boiling water; cool. Gradually add to cream cheese mixture, mixing until well blended. Pour over crust.

BAKE 10 min. Reduce oven temperature to 250°F. Bake 1 hour or until center is almost set. Run knife around rim of pan to loosen cake; cool before removing rim. Refrigerate 4 hours. Top with dollops of COOL WHIP and a sprinkle of additional cinnamon, if desired.

PHILADELPHIA New York-Style Strawberry Swirl Cheesecake

PREP: 15 min. | **TOTAL:** 5 hours 25 min. | **MAKES:** 16 servings.

- **1** cup graham cracker crumbs
- **3** Tbsp. sugar
- **3** Tbsp. butter, melted
- **5** pkg. (8 oz. each) PHILADELPHIA Cream Cheese, softened
- **1** cup sugar
- **3** Tbsp. flour
- **1** Tbsp. vanilla
- **1** cup BREAKSTONE'S or KNUDSEN Sour Cream
- **4** eggs
- **1/3** cup seedless strawberry jam

HEAT oven to 325°F.

LINE 13×9-inch pan with foil, with ends of foil extending over sides. Mix graham crumbs, 3 Tbsp. sugar and butter; press onto bottom of pan. Bake 10 min.

BEAT cream cheese, 1 cup sugar, flour and vanilla in large bowl with mixer until well blended. Add sour cream; mix well. Add eggs, 1 at a time, mixing on low speed after each just until blended. Pour over crust. Gently drop small spoonfuls of jam over batter; swirl with knife.

BAKE 40 min. or until center is almost set. Cool completely. Refrigerate 4 hours. Lift cheesecake from pan with foil handles before cutting to serve.

Substitute: Substitute 1 pkg. (16 oz.) frozen fruit, thawed, drained and pureed, for the 1/3 cup jam.

PHILADELPHIA 3-STEP Luscious Lemon Cheesecake

PREP: 10 min. | **TOTAL:** 3 hours 50 min. | **MAKES:** 8 servings.

---

2 pkg. (8 oz. each) PHILADELPHIA Cream Cheese, softened

½ cup sugar

½ tsp. grated lemon zest

1 Tbsp. fresh lemon juice

½ tsp. vanilla

2 eggs

1 ready-to-use graham cracker crumb crust (6 oz.)

HEAT oven to 350°F.

BEAT cream cheese, sugar, zest, juice and vanilla with electric mixer on medium speed until well blended. Add eggs; mix just until blended.

POUR into crust.

BAKE 40 min. or until center is almost set. Cool. Refrigerate 3 hours or overnight. Store leftover cheesecake in refrigerator.

Variation: Prepare as directed, substituting lime juice for the lemon juice and grated lime zest for the lemon zest.

Jazz It Up: Garnish with lemon peel before serving.

Chocolate-Orange Cheesecake

PREP: 20 min. | **TOTAL:** 6 hours 20 min. | **MAKES:** 16 servings.

20	chocolate wafers, finely crushed (about 1 cup)
¼	tsp. ground cinnamon
3	Tbsp. butter, melted
4	pkg. (8 oz. each) PHILADELPHIA Cream Cheese, softened
¾	cup sugar
½	cup BREAKSTONE'S or KNUDSEN Sour Cream
1	tsp. vanilla
4	eggs
1	pkg. (4 oz.) BAKER'S Semi-Sweet Chocolate, melted
2	Tbsp. orange-flavored liqueur
1	tsp. orange zest
½	cup orange marmalade

HEAT oven to 350°F.

MIX wafer crumbs, cinnamon and butter; press onto bottom of 9-inch springform pan.

BEAT cream cheese and sugar in large bowl with mixer until blended. Add sour cream and vanilla; mix well. Add eggs, 1 at a time, mixing on low speed after each just until blended. Transfer 3 cups batter to medium bowl; stir in melted chocolate. Pour over crust.

BAKE 30 min. Meanwhile, stir liqueur and zest into remaining batter; refrigerate until ready to use.

REDUCE oven temperature to 325°F. Spoon remaining batter over baked chocolate layer in pan; bake 30 min. or until center is almost set. Run small knife around rim of pan to loosen cake; cool before removing rim. Refrigerate cheesecake 4 hours. Top with marmalade just before serving.

GIFT-GIVING IDEAS

Easy Petit Fours

PREP: 5 min. | **TOTAL:** 5 min. | **MAKES:** 12 servings.

¼ cup PHILADELPHIA Strawberry Cream Cheese Spread

12 white fudge-covered sandwich cookies

6 strawberries, halved

1 oz. BAKER'S Semi-Sweet Chocolate, melted

SPREAD 1 tsp. cream cheese spread onto each cookie. Top each with strawberry half.

DRIZZLE with melted chocolate.

Chocolate-Raspberry Thumbprints

PREP: 20 min. | **TOTAL:** 45 min. | **MAKES:** 27 servings, 2 cookies each.

2 cups flour

1 tsp. baking soda

¼ tsp. salt

1 pkg. (4 oz.) BAKER'S Unsweetened Chocolate

½ cup butter

1 pkg. (8 oz.) PHILADELPHIA Cream Cheese, softened

1¼ cups sugar, divided

1 egg

1 tsp. vanilla

⅓ cup red raspberry jam

MIX flour, baking soda and salt; set aside. Microwave chocolate and butter in large microwaveable bowl on HIGH 2 min.; stir until chocolate is completely melted. Add cream cheese; stir until completely melted. Stir in 1 cup sugar, egg and vanilla. Add flour mixture; mix well. Refrigerate 15 min.

HEAT oven to 375°F. Roll dough into 1-inch balls; coat with remaining sugar. Place, 2 inches apart, on baking sheets. Press thumb into center of each ball; fill each indentation with about ¼ tsp. jam.

BAKE 8 to 10 min. or until lightly browned. Cool 1 min. on baking sheets; transfer to wire racks. Cool completely.

Pecan Tassies

PREP: 20 min. | **TOTAL:** 2 hours 15 min. | **MAKES:** 2 doz. or 24 servings.

---

4 oz. (½ of 8-oz. pkg.) PHILADELPHIA Cream Cheese, softened

½ cup butter or margarine, softened

1 cup flour

1 egg

¾ cup packed brown sugar

1 tsp. vanilla

¾ cup finely chopped PLANTERS Pecans

3 oz. BAKER'S Semi-Sweet Chocolate, melted

HEAT oven to 350°F.

BEAT cream cheese and butter in large bowl with mixer until well blended. Add flour; mix well. Refrigerate 1 hour or until chilled.

DIVIDE dough into 24 balls; place 1 in each of 24 miniature muffin pan cups. Press onto bottoms and up sides of cups to form shells. Beat egg in medium bowl. Add sugar and vanilla; mix well. Stir in nuts; spoon into pastry shells, filling each ¾ full.

BAKE 25 min. or until lightly browned. Let stand 5 min. in pans; remove to wire racks. Cool completely. Drizzle with melted chocolate. Let stand until firm.

Variation: For a quick garnish, dust cooled tarts with powdered sugar instead of drizzling with the melted chocolate.

Cheesecake Party Pops

PREP: 30 min. | **TOTAL:** 10 hours 45 min. | **MAKES:** 42 servings.

---

3 pkg. (8 oz. each) PHILADELPHIA Cream Cheese, softened

¾ cup sugar

1 tsp. vanilla

2 eggs

2 pkg. (4 oz. each) BAKER'S White Chocolate

2 pkg. (4 oz. each) BAKER'S Semi-Sweet Chocolate

HEAT oven to 325°F.

LINE 13×9-inch pan with foil, with ends of foil extending over sides. Beat cream cheese, sugar and vanilla with mixer until well blended. Add eggs, 1 at a time, mixing after each just until blended. Pour into prepared pan.

BAKE 35 min. or until center is set. Cool completely. Refrigerate 4 hours.

USE foil handles to lift cheesecake from pan before cutting into 42 squares. Roll each square into ball; place on parchment paper-covered baking sheet. Insert 1 lollipop stick into center of each. Freeze 4 hours.

MELT chocolates in separate bowls as directed on packages. Dip 21 lollipops in white chocolate; return to baking sheet. Repeat with remaining lollipops and semi-sweet chocolate. Drizzle remaining melted chocolate of contrasting color over lollipops. Refrigerate 1 hour or until chocolate is firm.

Peppermint Cookie Balls

PREP: 20 min. | **TOTAL:** 1 hour 30 min. | **MAKES:** 48 servings.

6 candy canes, finely chopped (about ⅓ cup), divided

1 pkg. (8 oz.) PHILADELPHIA Cream Cheese, softened

36 chocolate sandwich cookies, finely crushed

4 pkg. (4 oz. each) BAKER'S Semi-Sweet Chocolate, melted

RESERVE 1 Tbsp. chopped candy. Mix remaining candy with cream cheese and cookie crumbs until well blended.

SHAPE into 48 (1-inch) balls. Freeze 10 min. Dip balls in melted chocolate; place in single layer in shallow waxed paper-lined pan. Sprinkle with reserved candy.

REFRIGERATE 1 hour or until firm.

How to Store: Store in tightly covered container in refrigerator.